The Christmas Story

LET'S PLAY

The Christmas Story

Words and pictures by Leon Baxter

A LION BOOK

Here is the Christmas story. It is the story of Jesus' birthday.

One day, God sent an angel to tell Mary that she was going to have a baby.
He would be God's son.

When it was nearly time for the baby to be born, Mary and Joseph had to go to Bethlehem.

In Bethlehem, the innkeeper said, "There's no room in my house, but you can sleep in the stable."

The baby Jesus was born that night. Mary wrapped him in warm clothes and laid him in a manger to sleep.

Outside the town an angel told some shepherds that a special baby had been born. They came to see him.

Far away in another country, wise men saw a new star. It led them to the stable too. They brought Jesus presents of gold, frankincense and myrrh.

Shepherds, wise men and animals all came to see Jesus on that first Christmas night.

Help your child get more from this book

As well as reading this book aloud, why not encourage your child to try acting out the story?

Help your child think about their "part". How might it have felt to be one of the characters? What facial expression would they have had? What body language might they use? What might they have said? Use the child's understanding of a human character as a starting point to talk about the place of God in the story.

The picture at the start of this book shows some of the basic "props" needed to act out this story. Their use can be seen in each of the changing scenes of the book. These are only suggestions. If the right materials are not available most children will be happy to improvise.

If you have some time to spare, you can easily create simple support materials that will make acting the story more fun. Why not encourage your child to help with these? (The same materials could be used for Sunday school or classroom play.) Here are some ideas:

● Make an angel cloak by decorating an old sheet using cut potato shapes and yellow paint.

● Cut cardboard boxes into rock or bush shapes. These can be painted grey or green and placed along the route to

Bethlehem. Alternatively you could use cushions as rocks.

- Cut flaps in boxes of various sizes to represent doors in Bethlehem. Attach notices saying "Full" or "No Room".

- If suitable soft toys are not available, cut card shapes of sheep, cattle and donkeys (these can be free-standing or hand-held).

- Cut a large star shape from card and cover with foil. Suspend this from a stick by string. It can be carried in front of the wise men and then held above the stable area.

- Wrap a doll in cloth and place it in a small box to represent Jesus in the manger.

- Cut camels' heads from brown card. Dress their riders in dressing gowns to create the visiting wise men.

The fun of acting this story at home with friends and relations gathered for Christmas, or in a class group, will make this wonderful story even more memorable.

Published by
Lion Publishing plc
Sandy Lane West, Oxford, England
ISBN 0 7459 3745 4
Albatross Books Pty Ltd
PO Box 320, Sutherland, NSW 2232, Australia
ISBN 0 7324 1613 2

First edition 1995
First paperback edition 1997
10 9 8 7 6 5 4 3 2 1 0

A catalogue record for this book is available
from the British Library

Printed and bound in Malaysia